789 Elg

EDWARD ELGAR CENTENARY SKETCHES

Edited by

H. A. Chambers

NOVELLO AND COMPANY LTD.

160 WARDOUR STREET

LONDON, W.I

CONTENTS

Forty years with Elgar's music

Ever since I can remember—and my memories go back over 40 years now—I was regularly taken to the Henry Wood " Proms " and Sunday Concerts, and from the age of ten onwards the music of Edward Elgar has meant more to me than I can say. I never argue about him with people who try to point out his faults to me—if full-bloodedness, grandeur and nobility of melodic invention, can be termed " faults ". He has sometimes been called " vulgar "—and if there be any vulgarity in his music, it is of the kind that belongs to the greatest of artists, and you can find it in the same way at times in Verdi and Wagner.

Elgar's principal choral works are dealt with elsewhere in this brochure. I therefore propose within a short space to roam over the particular fields with which I have been associated as an orchestral player, soloist (I gave one of the earliest performances, after Felix Salmond, of the Cello Concerto with Sir Dan Godfrey in Bournemouth), chamber-music player and conductor.

As an orchestral player it was my good fortune to play under him on many occasions, and although he may not have been a great conductor in the professional sense of the term, anybody

sensitive to his music could not fail to glean a wonderful insight into how he wanted his music played—a lesson I hope I have never forgotten, for these occasions made a vivid and permanent impression on me. I well remember the last time he appeared at a Promenade Concert in the old Queen's Hall conducting his Second Symphony in a programme of British works, and how everything else in the programme was dwarfed by it.

Speaking as a cellist who performed his Concerto on many occasions, I can give the assurance that no writer of concertos has ever understood the instrument better, or scored for it with greater understanding and subtlety.

His chamber music, of which again I took part in many performances of the Quartet and Quintet, has never been appreciated at its true value, but I am sure the day will come when it will blossom fully into its own.

Of the choral works, I have so far only conducted *The Dream of Gerontius*—surely one of the greatest masterpieces of religious expression in music that our art can show. This great work is comparatively unknown in Europe despite the enthusiasm with which it was received at performances in Germany in 1901 and 1902. I hope it may be granted me, before I lay down my stick, to remedy this lamentable state of affairs.

JOHN BARBIROLLI

A Family Retrospect

ONE hundred years, and what memories that brings! All the stories of the struggle of the early years, of which I have heard so much that I feel I was actually there, and then the later years when the great career began and events moved from strength to strength to culminate in this wonderful celebration of 1957. It is strange to think that all the events of my father's career took place in a world that we should hardly recognize—no electricity, no road transport as we know it, no radio or television, no cinemas, no easy road to learning, such as the Teach Yourself books and a myriad others. Instead, it was the day of a more spacious and leisurely way of life in a country house. It is possible that all the modern 'improvements' would have handicapped rather than helped an ambitious student. However that may be, it was under the old conditions that this particular student had to contend and win through. It was through the deep study of books made known by his mother, who had a great love and knowledge of history and poetry, the proximity of the Cathedral and the Roman Catholic Church where he could listen at will and learn from the various services, and most practical of all, his father's shop where he could

examine the various instruments and learn about them at first hand, and also study the printed music.

What would my mother's feelings have been if she could have seen the world-wide recognition of his work in this centenary year? I can imagine her pride and satisfaction, for without her ambition and unfailing support at every turn, one wonders if he could have fulfilled himself to the same degree. She gave up her lifelong ambition to be a writer of note because she was so sure that a genius had been given into her charge, and it was her proud responsibility to keep from him every worry and difficulty as far as possible. It was she who made, with very little money, a home of which he could be proud and to which his friends could be invited; it was she who ruled the bar lines in all his scores and wrote in the choral parts when required, thereby saving him hours of manual labour; it was she who walked nearly two miles in sunshine or pouring rain to post the precious parcels of MSS. She was the only one who could understand every nuance of his musical intentions and who could, very gently, point out anything that did not absolutely satisfy her; and her advice was taken. Small wonder, then, that after her death inspiration left him and that after that time we have nothing really original. The few works

which did appear were taken from old sketch books of many years before. I can only hope that she does know and can share with us all in rejoicing and celebrating this wonderful year.

C. Elgar Blake

Composer as Conductor

Forty years or so ago it was not difficult to find someone who fancied himself (or herself) as an amateur musical critic who would unhesitatingly write off Edward Elgar as a " very poor conductor ". And yet, when pressed, they might be persuaded to admit that they could remember one or two very fine performances under his direction. Readers of Miss McVeagh's life will remember that when he came to live in London in 1912 he took over the greater part of the London Symphony Orchestra's Symphony Concert season, and conducted them on several tours which included, besides his own work, symphonies like Brahms's Third and Schumann's First, for which he had a special affection.

The conductors who were heard most in London at that time were Richter, Nikisch, Weingartner, and our own Wood and Ronald. It was not difficult to note that Elgar, although he had had a very great experience of music making in a number of different fields, had not had the day-to-day practice in the orchestral and choral world which had helped these five artists to their great positions. At the same time he was obviously a man of vast understanding with a fine critical faculty, which had been exercised in

many directions, not only musical, and he was the kind of man who could not contribute to anything without adding distinction to it.

And so, when he stood before a choir or orchestra, there was at once a deep respect, and his nervous, electric beat unfailingly added a tension and a lustre which produced a tone quality one came to recognize as highly personal. In particular one could go to a Three-Choir Festival confidently expecting exceptionally fine performances of most, if not all, the Elgar works in the programme.

I must justify this qualification. I think it was at Hereford one year that there had been a fine performance of *The Kingdom*. At its performance the following year it was at once apparent that the choir were perhaps resting too much on last year's laurels, and, in the enormous labour of preparing the long Festival programme, had not given *The Kingdom* quite its fair share of time. Bad intonation was evident near the start, and I felt that Sir Edward was losing interest, as he began to drive the performance, getting faster and faster, as if the one thing he wanted was to get out of the Cathedral and forget about music. We endured this for nearly an hour when we came to the wonderful scene " The sun goeth down", which was written for that great soprano, Agnes Nicholls. She had, if I remember rightly,

practically retired at that time, but returned at short notice to take over the part which she had made her own many years before. I shall never forget the intense concentration with which she began that gentle opening phrase, and the way the orchestra seemed instantly to spring to life and, immediately after, the disgruntled composer's interest quickened, and from that moment the performance returned to the extraordinary beauty of the year before. I have never, before or since, heard a solo singer's power of concentration change the whole feeling of a performance; control of this should be the conductor's business, but it is, I think, understandable that a composer-conductor can sometimes feel and give way to an irritation and a disappointment which a more hard-boiled executant could never allow himself. It would have been a professional conductor's job to pull things together when they showed signs of lapsing at the outset.

Musicians who heard Elgar conduct are getting fewer in number, but I think they will all agree that if they could make a list of the finest performances they had ever heard of Elgar's works, nearly, if not all of them, would turn out to have been conducted by Elgar himself.

ADRIAN C. BOULT

Publishing Office Memories

As a supplement to the more weighty matters dealt with by other writers in this brochure it may not be without interest to recall a few memories of direct contacts which members of the Novello publishing department had with Elgar. Naturally any notable composer will be closely associated with his publisher's executives, but in addition there are times when personal communication with the publishing office will be necessary, if only to deal with matters of detail.

A. J. Jaeger's close association with Elgar is, of course, on record, and is not surprising, for he possessed special qualities far beyond those needed for the successful management of a publishing department. Contrary to what has so often been suggested he was never the firm's official musical adviser. His work lay in the publishing office and involved responsibility for all the details inseparable from carrying out a general publishing programme. Much of this work must have been distasteful to a man of his highly developed musical culture. In due course, however, the soundness of his judgment was realized and respected, particularly in the encouragement and constructive criticism which he provided when he recognized creative talent. He

therefore became a kind of unofficial musical adviser to the firm, at any rate in the case of compositions outside the range of normal "bread and butter" publications. His unbounded admiration for, and belief in Elgar's work was exemplified by his complete refusal to accept as final the unfavourable criticisms which followed the first performance of *Gerontius* at Birmingham. He applied himself diligently to the task of proving that the Birmingham verdict was wrong, and it is largely due to his efforts that *Gerontius* has secured an established place in the repertory of oratorio.

All this will be familiar to anyone who has read an Elgar biography. It is restated here in order to emphasize the mutual esteem and close friendship which had developed between the composer and the publishing office manager, and which the former, some years before *Gerontius,* had so movingly expressed by "Nimrod" in the *Enigma Variations*.

When the present writer entered the publishing office as a junior in 1907 Jaeger had retired, a very sick man, and although he lived until 1909 his work was done. His unique qualities could not be matched by any successor. As a consequence Elgar's direct relations with the publishing office became more infrequent and less personal in character, but they were always

marked by his inherent courteousness and freedom from any suggestion of " side ".

One small incident is permanently fixed in
my mind. I was detailed to meet the composer at
Paddington station and take from him the score
of a movement from one of the Symphonies—I
cannot now recall whether it was the First (1908)
or the Second (1911). When Elgar came off the
train he said there was still a little to do, and
asked me to go home with him to Severn House,
Hampstead. On the journey by cab he was
perusing the score. At home he proceeded
rapidly to add the finishing touches, and then,
turning to the piano, he played a fragment here
and another there, with an occasional remark,
for all the world as if I had been a qualified
musician instead of a publishing office junior.
I left the house with a feeling that several cubits
had been added to my stature.

The system of having proofs read in the
office and corrected before being sent to a composer aimed at relieving him of the task of marking typographical errors. In some cases, too, any
musical point which occurred to the reader
would be referred to the composer. Such queries
were frequently concerned with musical sole-
cisms which in those days were rarely allowed to
pass unchallenged. Elgar, of course, was seldom
troubled with questions of this kind. He knew

exactly what he wanted, and although he was no slavish adherent to musical orthodoxy it seemed natural for him to express his ideas without caus- ing the pundits of his day to raise their eyebrows too high. This applied particularly to his vocal part-writing which, whatever its complexity, rarely departed from grammatical purity. When he did ignore text-book precepts he did so not from caprice or carelessness but doubtless because he considered it necessary in order to produce the effect he wanted. An occasional query in his proofs was almost invariably accepted as being constructive rather than pedantic criticism, and received a straightforward answer.

There was one occasion, however, when an over-zealous proof reader put his foot in it. In 1909 Elgar was asked to contribute to a collection of *New Cathedral Psalter Chants* then in preparation. In one of the chants the reader noticed consecu- tive fifths between alto and bass. Marking the offending notes with parallel lines, he wrote on the proof " ? intended ". Elgar's marginal reply was terse and to the point: " Yes! if you don't like them leave the chant out. E. E."

Among Novello's proof readers and re- visers at this time was H. Elliot Button. In the course of his work of preparing manuscripts for the press he was continually contending with the haphazard way in which composers wrote their

music. He therefore set out to formulate some general principles of notation, and these were embodied in a primer, *System in Musical Notation,* which was published in 1919. Elgar, who confessed to being fascinated by printing and all that belongs to it, was much interested in Button's precepts, although he did not always go the whole way with the author. Nevertheless he was always ready to accept suggestions when he found them good. His general approval of the Button system was contained in a most entertaining preface which he contributed to the primer, in which he expressed a sense of gratitude to the author " for materially improving the ' complection ' of some efforts of my own ".

The output of Elgar's major works ended in 1919 with the Cello Concerto. The twelve preceding years had seen the production of the Violin Concerto, the two Symphonies, *Falstaff,* and two choral works, *The Spirit of England* and *The Music Makers,* the last named making use of themes from the composer's other works.

During this period the knowledge that a new Elgar work was in the press aroused in many quarters much curiosity as to what was in store. Sometimes this was an embarrassment to the publishing office. It was the practice to have two sets of proofs from the engravers, one for the readers, the other for reference. One gentleman

in particular, a most enthusiastic Elgarian, seemed to have the freedom of the house, and was inclined to wander into the publishing office in the hope of seeing something of interest. Any Elgar proofs were irresistible and were apt to be irregularly " borrowed " for examination. Many a time were such proofs hastily put out of sight when the treasure-hunter was known to be about.

Of the Novello staff who met the composer personally hardly any now remain. The few who do, and they are no more than two or three at most, were only concerned with trivialities compared with the close understanding between Elgar and Jaeger. Nevertheless there remains a feeling of satisfaction in having had personal contact with the great English composer and a share, however small, in the publication of some of his greatest works.

H. A. CHAMBERS

An American Voice

THROUGHOUT my musical career the music of Elgar has been a constant source of joy and inspiration. For in conducting his music, one was left with the feeling of exhilaration and excitement that only great music can bestow. And as a composer, the study of his music has been a deep and satisfying experience, and at the same time has served as a lesson from a superb master. It is from these two points of view that I should like to put down my impressions and observations.

I have always felt that one of the reasons why the bulk of Elgar's music is so little performed outside of England lies in that most mysterious sense that a conductor must have for the flexibility and nuances of tempo which it demands. His works almost seem to perish if a rigid tempo is imposed upon them. This seems to me to arise from the essential nervousness, and at the same time the utmost poetic feeling, with which his music is so generously imbued. The tempo variations that arise in the course of an Elgar work are so subtle and elastic that they demand from the conductor and performer an almost complete infatuation with the music. For Elgar's music will not play by itself;

merely to supervise it and give it professional routine playing will only serve to immobilize it.

It may well be, in the *Enigma Variations,* that the problem is more readily understood by conductors of different nationality and musical background owing to the shortened musical form, while his music of extended length, such as the symphonies and *Falstaff,* has remained a closed book. If conductors would only realize that these works, too, demand the same fluidity that the *Enigma* demands, there would be no difficulty at all in achieving a more universal audience for Elgar's music.

In the United States, the works of Elgar most frequently heard are the *Enigma,* the Violin and Cello Concertos and, occasionally, the *Cockaigne Overture,* and it is only when one of the distinguished British conductors is in charge that we are treated to any of the other works.

The reasons for the neglect of *Falstaff,* I feel, are even more complex, for this unique work demands very special understanding and listening on the part of the audience. First of all, besides the arduous and exacting musical demands that it makes upon the conductor and performers, the audience must bring an understanding of the play to it. I am given to understand that even in England this work is not too often performed, and this gap between the music and the literary

awareness of the audience has yet to be bridged, although Sir John Barbirolli has attempted to overcome the problem by first giving an illustrated lecture before playing the work. If this work presents so many problems to an English audience, one can well imagine how alien it must seem to an American one.

It is my personal feeling that *Falstaff* remains Elgar's supreme orchestral work, in spite of the special difficulty it presents of relating the music to the understanding of the audience. It is only to be regretted that he did not do an opera on the subject, for then all the problems that confront the orchestral version would have evaporated in the opera house.

However, there is another aspect to *Falstaff*, which is, of course, that the work may also be regarded almost as a portrait of Elgar. I have always felt that the enigma of the *Variations* was not a musical one, but rather a personal attitude. Each variation is a variation on an enigmatic theme—the enigma of the composer himself. And so, in *Falstaff* as well, we have a portrait in many ways of the composer: his deep sense of the country scene and pastoral tranquillity, his enjoyment of ceremony and pomp, his intellectual cynicism and, at the same time, emotional unity with his fellow-man. All these are not only a part of Elgar, but a part of *Falstaff*.

It is, however, in the Second Symphony that Elgar achieved, perhaps, his most intimate and personal expression, particularly in the first movement, which I feel is unlike any other opening movement of any symphony ever written. For this movement, with its vibrancy and ecstatic flood tide of sound and the great urgencies of its innumerable lyrical themes, brings to my mind the Spring landscapes of Van Gogh and Samuel Palmer. Its embracing of joy and delight, which he wished to capture, have certainly resulted in a most unique and personal vision.

One could go on to describe the transparency and pliant quality of his orchestral technique, and one could devote many pages to the skill and ingenuity of his counterpoint and harmonic subtleties, but to me one of the most splendid things about this music is the pleasure and joy that sweeps over the faces of the players as one of the great climaxes of his music is reached. This certainly is one of the finest tributes that can be paid to a composer.

To have lived with and studied and performed Elgar's music has been more than a great musical experience—it has been an enriching of one's whole life, for it brings in its train not only melodies and harmonies that remain permanently in one's memory, but also a great tranquillity and solace, and at the same time the

joy and excitement of being on a mountain peak. For Elgar's music is, in the end, an affirmation of the miracle of life and never a negation of it. This accomplishment certainly places him with the very greatest of the masters of music.

BERNARD HERRMANN

The Apostles
and The Kingdom

As I gaze at my bookshelves and see all the books that have been written about Edward Elgar I wonder if there is any more to be said to throw further light on this great figure in English music; yet there has been so little said of the two important oratorios, *The Apostles* and *The Kingdom*, compared with writings about his more popular works, that one must pause for a moment and consider them.

It is true that studies of their technicalities phrase by phrase have appeared, trying to prove without doubt that their composition cannot be compared with *The Dream of Gerontius, Enigma Variations,* the two Symphonies, etc. Do the studies of these two works really take us much farther than laying bare Elgar's method in assembling them? Have we ever tried to ignore the ' how ' and concentrate on *why* they were written? Where did Elgar stand at the moment of their conception?

He had completed *The Dream of Gerontius* after years of thought and study; it had been launched—perhaps not very successfully—but was now getting under way with performances

of greater worth. He knew that it was far above any choral work he had yet composed, for, after all, did he not say " This is the best of me ". A man in the middle forties, who makes such a statement does not do so with the thought that he has attained the topmost pinnacle, and can now rest. He feels that he has reached the top of the particular peak he has been exploring, and must now look around for greater heights to conquer; in short, he would be considering where to turn next. He probably realised that *The Dream of Gerontius* was now on the way to becoming a great success but that its main appeal might be only to those of the Catholic Faith.

It is well known that Elgar liked writing music for " the people ". He had just completed the *Pomp and Circumstance* Marches and *Cockaigne*.

What would be more natural than that for his next oratorio he should turn to some Bible story known to everybody? Thus was born *The Apostles* in 1903. The work did not win great favour in this country; the critics did not acclaim it; performances were few, perhaps owing to the lukewarm reception, perhaps owing to the cost of production. Therefore audiences did not have the opportunity of becoming familiar with it. Twenty years after its composition a critic wrote —" *The Apostles* presents exceptional difficulties in performance; it is rare to hear a really satisfactory

interpretation of the work "—and he went on to explain that to capture its spirit " singers and players must know the whole score—not merely their own thread of notes."

The Kingdom followed soon after *The Apostles* in 1906, and although the score is not quite so complicated, the same intimacy between singers and players is necessary.

It is generally agreed that both Oratorios are difficult for an audience to absorb at first hearing, and familiarity is needed to make them live for the public. In one town in England it has been customary to perform these works fairly frequently since 1920. At first, audiences were small, but as the years went on and the war period arrived, while other works drew moderate attendances, hundreds of people were turned away when *The Apostles* and *The Kingdom* were performed. People found these works so soul satisfying that they gained a spiritual uplift which helped them through the dark days.

It is curious to note that during the last war, whereas most Choral Societies which remained active did so by performances of *Messiah, Elijah*, etc., one Society could do so only by performing the Elgar works.

The two works are linked together in more ways than one. *The Apostles* deals with the period when Jesus was on earth, and closes with

His Ascension; *The Kingdom* carries on the story, and tells of the Church in Jerusalem. Elgar has used so many themes from the first work in the second, that they seem to be one gigantic structure. They should be performed as such, but so far it is doubtful if anyone has ventured to do so.

I first met Elgar in 1909 when taking part in a performance of *The Kingdom* under his direction. The chorus had rehearsed the work for nearly a year, so their part was pretty well known. I shall never forget Elgar's striking personality, nor the spiritual atmosphere he engendered. His works have never sounded quite the same as when he conducted them. The impact of that performance is something I shall always remember. Its inspiration made me continue to study the work, though opportunities of hearing it were few; those that were to be heard convinced me that here was a work which, if studied long and devotedly, would repay a hundredfold. What of the effect of these works on Elgar himself?

He heard so many matter-of-fact performances in which the spirit was absent that he despaired of the future of his choral works, and in one of his letters said, "There is not a single voice coming on in the 'solo' world, and young people have quite given up choral work." Some of our musicologists have tried to find the reason

for the rise and fall in quality of Elgar's output.
The first World War undoubtedly put the brake
on, but the death of his wife in 1920 was so severe
a blow that it is understandable that for a period
he felt he could do no more.

The spirit of man has strong powers of
recuperation, and in the late 1920's and early
1930's he seemed to have recovered a lot of his
buoyancy. In the Spring of 1933 Elgar conducted
a performance of *The Apostles* (probably the last
one under his direction), and although because
of his infirmity he had to sit down to conduct, the
rehearsal seemed to put him in good spirits. At
the performance Elgar became more and more
lost in the music. A slow smile came over his
face, and he almost stopped conducting; his
spirit seemed to have taken wings. Had it not
been for the usual alertness of Billy Reed, who
was leading the orchestra, and who literally kept
the performance together until Elgar came out
of his dream, there might have been complete
breakdown. When Elgar left the rostrum it was
obvious that he was greatly moved.

It is well known that when questioned
about the concluding part of the trilogy, Elgar
always changed the subject. At a reception after
this performance he replied, " We shall have to
think of that." It may have been that his
thoughts had turned for a moment to those

sketches in the cupboard; but it was not to be, for in a few months he was dead.

May it not be, in what has been set down here, there is a clue to the reason why *The Apostles* and *The Kingdom* were not followed by greater and still greater choral works?

Though it is too late to think of that now, it is not too late for a revival in interest in *The Apostles* and *The Kingdom*. In the past seven years there have been in this country 146 performances of *The Dream*, 14 of *The Apostles* and 34 of *The Kingdom*.

It is a great pity that the gramophone companies could not be persuaded to record these works before Elgar died, and while the singers and players who had absorbed the Elgar idiom were still with us. It is understandable that the economic factor was the stumbling block, but it would have required very little of the public money that has been set aside for music. The cost of presenting these works to the public is considerable, and choral societies, very naturally, are frightened of the possible loss if they do not draw adequate audiences. One wonders from time to time whether it might be possible to produce an edition requiring a reduced orchestra to help choral societies which have adequate vocal forces, but cannot afford the Elgar orchestra. This is a suggestion that will make the purists hold up their hands in horror;

certainly the effect could not equal that of the original score. One feels, however, that if something could be done to make these two works better known, it would be a worth-while effort in the cause of choral singing in this country.

ALAN J. KIRBY

Impressions—
Musical and Personal

Benign, lovable, extremely generous, and with an almost nonchalant attitude towards the music he created—so do I remember Sir Edward Elgar. His was the voice of England, and as a human being he was the very embodiment of all that is most characteristic of the British. Sustained by the traditions that bore him, his roots deep in his native soil, he seemed utterly relaxed. His music belonged to England, and he belonged to that happy generation of composers who had no need to defend their musical creations against a hostile world.

Although events have carried us a long way from the stately security and the staunch forthrightness of which his music speaks, his countrymen never fail to be stirred by the almost atavistic chord Elgar's music strikes.

Through Elgar's music I instinctively grasped, as a boy of sixteen, his English qualities, which I have since come to admire and understand in this island race. Our very first meeting established this warmth and sympathy, although in a most unexpected way. I had come with some trepidation to face a living composer after only a

few weeks' study of his Violin Concerto. I was prepared to be stopped at every bar, to be corrected
and to be initiated into a style of which this was
my first example. Instead, I had played but a few
bars when this sunny and jovial gentleman in
tweed coat announced that he saw no need for
me to continue, and that, as for himself, he was
most anxious to be off to the races on that sunny
summer's day in 1932. We did not meet again until
the recording session a few days later when I too
found myself carried along by the wave of sympathy and feeling which rose from the body of
musicians who understood him so well that he
hardly had to exert himself in the usual manner
of conductors.

I was anxious that he should encounter
the same understanding from both musicians
and audience when later we gave the first performance of the Concerto in Paris. To that end,
Georges Enesco, who was conducting the rest
of the concert, devoted himself most selflessly
and thoroughly rehearsed the orchestra in two
long sessions. When Sir Edward took over the
third rehearsal, as a deliberate preparation for the
performance, he found the same acceptance and
response as he had received from his own
musicians in England.

Curiously enough, my recollection gains
at least as much from the breakfasts we enjoyed

at our home in Ville d'Avray in the outskirts of Paris, where he would receive at my mother's hand his onion soup, as from our experience on the concert platform. He was always the same man under these varying circumstances.

YEHUDI MENUHIN

The Music Maker

My first meeting with Edward Elgar and his wife arose from a friendship, begun early in 1895, between myself and Miss Mary Frances Baker, who, a few months later, became my stepmother. Following a visit to my father and me at the Rectory, Wolverhampton, Miss Baker took me back with her to Gloucestershire, to her house near her brother's home, at Hasfield. Her brother was William Meath Baker, who became "W.M.B." of the *Enigma Variations*. It was during this visit that I first heard about Edward Elgar.

Among Miss Baker's friends was Miss Caroline Alice Roberts who used to live near Hasfield but had now gone to live at Malvern. It was on a visit to her there that Miss Baker found her friend vigorously practising on the piano, and learnt that she was having accompaniment lessons from a Mr. Elgar who was teacher of the violin at Worcester High School. This professional association developed into a romance and their engagement was soon announced. Their wedding took place at the Brompton Oratory in May, 1889.

Shortly after my father's marriage to Miss Baker, my stepmother and I went to the station

at Wolverhampton to meet Mr. and Mrs. Elgar, who were coming from Malvern for the day to see their old friend in her new home. The two friends fell into one another's arms, and Mr. Elgar was left for me to look after. Of course I was longing to hear about music, but he wanted to know when he could go and see the Wolverhampton Wanderers play football.

"Not today, I'm afraid; they don't play here on Fridays—Saturday is their day here as a rule." "Oh! well, next time I come here I shall come on a Saturday; will you take me to a match?" Of course I would, and did so the next Spring.

After luncheon that day we had coffee in the drawing room and at once he noticed the piano (my stepmother's Pleyel). "Why—there's the black piano! Let's see how its inside has stood the move!" And he sat down and began to play. I just stood stockstill where I was, it sounded so different from ordinary playing. Then he took a score of some sort out of his pocket and set it up on the piano. To see what it was I drifted over towards the piano and stood by it, turning over for him as he went on. It was quite straight-forward at first, but soon I noticed that other things were being put in which were not on the printed page. However, I seemed to make no mistake and in a few minutes he stopped, shut

up the score and put it away. It struck me afterwards that I had been through—and seemed to
have passed—a sort of examination. In later years
I often remembered that day. Faced with an
almost blank page of music-paper with perhaps a
few pencilled notes on it, I was expected to turn
over at the right time when he was playing some
full orchestral passage, covering apparently the
whole keyboard. I often wondered how many
mistakes I made. He never scolded or laughed; he
just went on, and I went on too, with great joy,
hoping for the best.

It has been suggested that the name
Elgar, which sounds rather un-English, is of
Scandinavian origin. It may be so, for East Kent
was full of Elgars in the sixteenth-eighteenth cen-
turies, and the effect of trade in a county so
situated geographically was certain to bring in
many foreigners.

In 1948, my husband asked Elgar's daughter
(Mrs. Elgar Blake) if she would like him to trace
her father's Kentish ancestry, and we found our-
selves faced with a formidable problem. The pages
of the registers at St. Mary's Church, Dover, were
full of the name Elgar and no less than four
different families of Elgar were living in Dover
in the nineteenth century. However, these
beautifully kept registers had a column on every
page giving the profession or trade of male

parents and we were soon on the track. After some weeks of work and motoring all over South-East Kent we were able to trace Edward Elgar's male-line pedigree back five generations to the marriage of Henry Elgar, at Saltwood, in 1712.

These men all married Kentish women whose names are common to the locality, which indicates that Elgar's father was as English as anyone can expect to be in this country of mixed races.

The Elgar pedigree, which has been registered at the College of Arms, now hangs at Elgar House, Broadheath, near Worcester, where Elgar was born in 1857.

But to skip back again sixty years: What was Elgar like to know in those days? A most interesting and delightful character, witty and full of fun. He had a wonderful gift for repartee, "impossible" answers and ridiculous quotations. You had no chance ever of getting the last word. I was so often beaten for an answer because I was laughing too much to speak. Meals were often a trial as one was afraid of choking, and it didn't help much when Mrs. Elgar, at the other end of the table, said, in great disapproval, "Oh Edward dear, really!" All he said was "Cheer up, chicky!" I remember very well a small luncheon party when in the general laughter which followed one of his outrageous remarks he was heard to remark that if no one ate anything—it was cheaper!

But there were days when he was moody
and depressed—things had been disappointing and
people tiresome, and he was very quiet—" Sick
to death of mouldy music " and " going to give it
all up ". " Have you brought your bicycle? Oh!
come on, let's go out somewhere. " So out we
went and sat by the river, watching for things—
birds, butterflies and dragonflies—and very soon
the mood passed and all was better. He used
to say " Music is in the air, and I take what I
want. " I remember particularly a lovely summer day at Hereford. We had gone out on
our bicycles and somewhere near Holme Lacy
went down to the River Wye and sat down on the
bank among the wild flowers. Occasionally, he
would put up a finger—" Something moving over
there, do you see it?" He was very silent, all the
way home, and he went straight to the study
and began playing the piano. He had left the
door open—which meant that I could follow
him in if I wanted to. I leaned against a table and
watched him and wondered what such lovely
music could be about—the beauty of the day and
of the scene by the river? Yes—but far more than
that. I always wondered how, with only four
fingers and a thumb on each hand, he managed
to make the sounds that he did. At last, I stole
out of the room and sat on the stairs to listen. He
scolded me for that afterwards, but I told him I was

afraid of being a disturbance and breaking the spell.

Apart from his great musical gifts Elgar was really quite a normal person. I never knew him fly off the handle or use bad language. He invented a vocabulary of " swear-words " which he used with great effect, only it was so comic that one had to laugh, which usually made him crosser still. One day I was sitting on the floor in the study at " Craeglea ", and he was picking out a passage in *Gerontius* on the trombone—he didn't always produce the note he wanted and I laughed aloud. He remarked, wrathfully, " How do you expect me to play this dodgasted thing if you laugh?" So I cleared out and sat on the stairs where I could laugh in peace. When he did it again I went away downstairs to see if I could help Mrs. Elgar with something. I told her why I'd come and she and I both laughed together.

As a matter of fact he was really a very well-controlled person. He did not smoke excessively, and drank very moderately. As any one may see from Dr. Young's book of Elgar Letters, he had a considerable command of words and he was fairly widely read. He had a natural liking for puzzles of various sorts and was good at solving them. With this there went a certain mental preciseness which is exemplified by the care with which any notes on his works were compiled, as,

for instance, those written for the programme of
the first performance of the *Enigma Variations*.

Like all sensitive people he was inclined to
swing between elation and depression. It is easy
to make too much of this—particularly of the
depression. I have seen these phases many times
and they seldom lasted very long. Like a great
many other people, he could, at times, be very
tiresome, but even that was seldom important.
Sometimes, if he saw that the ' tiresomeness '
was becoming boring, he would vary it. In one
matter, strangely perhaps, he was very consistent.
He did not like talking about music, with
the result that casual visitors, who naturally
expected the conversation to be about music,
frequently went away disappointed or even
irritated. This reluctance to discuss music was
shelved in the case of his Lectures, as Professor of
Music at Birmingham University. There is some
good, hard sense to be found in these utterances,
but the Press was critical, and the Lectures are now
rarely mentioned.

But of course, the memories which I prize
most are of hearing so much of Elgar's greater
music played to me long before publication.

To have turned over for him by the hour
together sketches for *Gerontius,* the two Oratorios,
both the Symphonies and the Violin Concerto—
from pencil sketch to printed proof— it was, all

of it, so absorbingly interesting. And this covers
ten years of Elgar's greatest creative ability.
Speaking of my experiences chronologically, I
should have mentioned the *Variations* first, but
my hearing of them for the first time was quite
different from the other music that I heard. The
Variations was a sort of family joke and it had been
kept from me entirely until that day in November,
1898, when I sat down to turn over the finished
piano score. What *was* this? I saw the initials of
several people I knew, and the music was almost
like portraits, so cleverly had they been drawn.
Mrs. Elgar's lovely *C.A.E.* portrait—how had
he made it so like her? (I did not find that out till
years afterwards!) Some of the friends were
caricatured: *R.B.T.* (No. III) in particular—Elgar
roared with laughter and so did I; *W.M.B.*
(No. IV) and his sharp, decisive giving of orders;
and, later, *Troyte* (No. VII), his great friend
Troyte Griffith, and his arguing! That Variation
seems to end—" But, my good chap, can't you
SEE? " followed by a violent passage right down
the piano. I shall never forget the noise we made
that afternoon.

Elgar was clearly pleased with what he had
done and undoubtedly it was extremely clever.

Then, at No. IX we had the lovely *Nimrod* (and his beloved Beethoven!), dedicated to
A. J. Jaeger, of Novello's. So lovely did I think it

that when Elgar got to the end I sat back and did
not turn over. I thought it must be the end of
the work. But Elgar said, " Go on, turn over ";
so I turned over and saw on the next page No. X,
Dorabella. When he finished it I simply did
not know what to say. A complete surprise, a
high honour and a very great joy. Mrs. Elgar
came to my rescue from her chair by the fireside
—" Isn't it lovely? Dora dear, I do *hope* you like
it?" ("Like it? " I should think I did, and do.)

Another most wonderful memory is of
the day at Birchwood, near Malvern, in 1899, when
I heard " Praise to the Holiest " for the first time.
When Elgar had finished playing that particular
section in Part II of *Gerontius,* again I did not know
what to say, and I sat silent. At last I think I
murmured " How perfectly wonderful ". But
he said nothing—his mind was far away, on the
music and what the orchestra would be sounding
like. He got out a pipe and lighted it. Then he
turned to me—" How does that strike you? "
Just imagine being asked such a thing! What
could I say? Then, something came back into my
mind: I had noticed the peculiar way in which the
music had seemed to go *piano* and then *forte* again,
not quite in accord with the words; so, greatly
daring, I ventured: "It makes me think of great
doors opening and shutting." Elgar turned round
and faced me, and, for a moment, I wondered if

I had said something dreadful. " Does it? " he said, " That is exactly what I mean. "

I heard a good deal of *The Apostles* in 1902-3, and how I loved it! I would rather hear it than any other of Elgar's choral works. I shall never forget the beauty of the first performance at Birmingham in 1903. The chorus, having mastered by that time the Elgar idiom and done wonderful work under their new chorus-master, W. H. Wilson, had the advantage of being conducted by the composer. The chief solo part was taken by Ffrangçon-Davies (who used to speak of it as " the part of the Christus "), and his supreme mastery made the performance a miracle of beauty and understanding. As to Elgar, his conducting that day established him in the musical world as the finest conductor of his own choral works.

I also heard sketches and finished parts of *The Kingdom* at Hereford in 1905, and heard, with Lady Elgar after hours of patient waiting, " The Sun Goeth Down " played on the piano for the first time at about 2 a.m.

And last, in 1909, I heard the finished Violin Concerto, which I thought almost more beautiful than anything else. How he managed to get the Cadenza over to me *on a piano* was almost beyond belief, but, as he played, I seemed to see the Elysian Fields and part of what was there, and it made me cry. Later, at the time of the

Gloucester Festival, I heard Elgar and Kreisler going through the Concerto behind locked doors! They had locked themselves in a bedroom with a piano, and I sat on the stairs outside and listened. Kreisler was trying bits of the solo part and I heard the two men struggling with each other's language; then more playing, and a burst of approval from the composer.

Then they came down to tea. I had hoped to hear the Concerto discussed, but no. Sitting down to the table Elgar began at once—" Did you see what the local paper said about the Missionaries being seen off at Foregate Street Station, Dorabella?" "No," I said, "what happened?" "The paper described how a large crow on the platform sang a hymn!"

I finish, as I have often finished " talks " on Elgar: He was like several people rolled into one and you never knew till you arrived which one you were going to see.

DORA M. POWELL

Elgar's Light Music

It is perhaps the hallmark of the really great composer that, while the bulk of his music may be above the heads of many of his hearers, he has the ability to write music which everybody can like, love and hum, whistle or strum. To me Sibelius and Elgar are the two best examples of twentieth-century composers with a real gift for deliberately writing immediately likeable music for their fellow countrymen. One of the pleasures of a broadcasting conductor's life is that, through radio's insatiable demands for a wide range of pieces, he has the opportunity of conducting music which can hardly ever find a place in public concert-halls where even the best light music is nowadays almost taboo. Only Sir Thomas Beecham, that king of light music conductors, dare play what he calls his " R.P.O. Lollipops ". At one time Elgar's best known example of light music was his opus 12, *Salut d'Amour,* published in 1889, and eventually arranged and re-arranged for a marvellous and strange list of instrumental combinations. It was not Elgar's fault if many of the people who played it nauseated their listeners by their glutinous phrasing and commonplace rubato. Played sensitively and according to Elgar's score, I find it still a likeable piece.

But this was by no means his first piece of music in popular vein. He had published in 1884 a piece in the Spanish style called *Sevillana,* opus 7, the ebullient scoring of which is extraordinarily characteristic of his later music. I have enjoyed conducting it on several occasions and one section of it is amusingly more reminiscent of Waldteufel than of Seville. But his three pieces forming opus 10, published in 1889, are more refined. Though scored for full orchestra with four horns, they are ingeniously cued for single woodwind, two horns, one trumpet (or cornet), drums and strings. The young composer, doubtless with a good deal of experience in working with amateur orchestras near his birthplace, says, " Any other instrument in the score may be added with corresponding gain in effect ". There is an attractive Mazurka; a charming though not very Moorish *Sérénade Mauresque,* in G minor ending rather surprisingly on the dominant; and an excellent piece called *Contrasts* in which he contrasts a pastiche of the gavotte A.D. 1700 with a very Elgarian gavotte of A.D. 1900.

Elgar wrote several minuets, a dance rhythm that seemed rather specially to appeal to him. There is one in the first *Wand of Youth* Suite; in his opus 21 for small orchestra (1899) originally composed for piano in 1897; in *The Crown of India* music; in his incidental music to the play *Beau*

Brummel and in the *Severn Suite* for brass band. But in none of them did he seem to write anything very characteristic of himself.

Though in their original form his *Scenes from the Bavarian Highlands,* opus 27, published in 1896, were written for chorus and orchestra with words by his wife, three of them, slightly adapted to be playable with orchestra alone, have become a welcome addition to the repertoire of light orchestral suites, and the "Lullaby" (In Hammersbach) is a constantly heard piece in light radio programmes where its freshness often stands forth among more brash music like a good deed in a naughty world. Something of the same serene, open-air feeling pervades his opus 15, *Chanson de Nuit* and *Chanson de Matin,* published in 1901. Both are really beautiful. *Chanson de Nuit* is a deeply expressive slow melody for the violins on the G string exquisitely orchestrated. *Chanson de Matin* is blithe and dewy-eyed.

Perhaps there is one field of light music in which Elgar shines more than any of his rivals and that is in the world of marches. Sousa said that he would rather be the composer of a good march than of a bad symphony, and it is certainly true that there are few composers of good marches who can claim credit for more than one each. Elgar's first essay was the *Imperial March,* opus 32, composed in 1897, and though it is not

uncharacteristic of the composer it was soon
overshadowed by the first of his five *Pomp and
Circumstance* marches which set an absolutely new
note in the world of marches, a note which can
only be described as Elgarian and which was so
overwhelming in its effect that any composer
nowadays who has to write a march for a cere-
monial occasion seldom succeeds in doing more
than writing another *Pomp and Circumstance,* as we
were forcibly reminded during the Coronation
Year of Queen Elizabeth. It is easy to forget now
how very original was the style of the *Pomp and
Circumstance* marches. The first four were written
between 1904 and 1907 but the fifth, the only one in
6/8 time, did not appear until 1930 and in between
he had written three other marches: a vivid and
rather strangely fantastic one to begin his second
Wand of Youth Suite; one for the Coronation of
1911 which is more of a Processional March,
some of it in 3/4 time; and an *Empire March* for
the opening of the Wembley Exhibition in 1924,
which never seems to be thought worth reviving.

Much of Elgar's light music has a wistful,
dreamlike, tender quality which is perhaps first
demonstrated in his opus 43, *Dream Children,* published in 1902, two delightfully contrasted pieces
inspired by one of Charles Lamb's essays. There
is much of this dreamlike quality in the little
piece for small orchestra *Canto popolare* (In Moon-

light), extracted from his Concert Overture *In the South*, opus 50 (1904), a genuinely moving treatment of a snatch of an Italian folk song, which has some additional moments of beauty not actually found in the larger work. Later in life Elgar similarly published two delicate extracts from his Symphonic Study *Falstaff—Jack Falstaff, Page to the Duke of Norfolk* and *Gloucestershire: Shallow's Orchard*—and of course *Nimrod* and *Dorabella* from the *Enigma Variations* are often played separately.

But this wistful dreamlike quality was most fully revealed when the composer published in 1907 and 1908 his two Suites from the play *The Wand of Youth*, which he had composed for members of his family when he was fourteen years of age. Elgar in his late forties still seemed to be able to feel the boyish freshness of his embryonic music in spite of the mastery of orchestral technique he had acquired. Was ever more delightful light music written than *Moths and Butterflies* with its hovering fanciful phrases for the violins; *The Little Bells* with the contrasting bigger bell in the middle section, which he later used in his incidental music to *The Starlight Express* (1915); the charming *Slumber Scene* with the bass part written for the three open strings of the old double bass so that his young sister could take part in the orchestra; the *Sun Dance* with the flitting lights which were flashed in the eyes of the old people with the

aid of mirrors, and the *Fountain Dance* with the jets
rising and falling; the dreamlike *Fairy Pipers* with
the characteristic rubato phrase for the clarinets;
and, perhaps most endearing of all, the Bears—
Tame Bear, with a picture of the pathetic bear being
taken around on a lead to dance in the streets,
and *The Wild Bears*, one of the most enjoyable of
all orchestral romps which no orchestra can
resist, with its vividly descriptive long growls in
the bass department?

After this Elgar wrote very little light music
of a quality to compare with his early works. *The
Crown of India*, opus 66 (1912), though well written
seems not to have the appeal to encourage many
performances either complete or in extracts
nowadays. *The Dance of Nautch Girls* in 3/8 time has
some characteristic phrases; there is a brilliant
Warriors' Dance and *The March of the Mogul Emperors*
is more like a Purcellian or Handelian hornpipe.
The *Severn Suite*, which he composed for brass
band in 1930 and re-scored for full orchestra in
1932, does not seem to have made much headway
either. But one late work did have an immediate
success when it was composed in 1931, his *Nursery
Suite*, opus 87, written for the Queen (then Princess
Elizabeth) and her Sister. After a very great
initial success with forty performances in the
first year, it was used by Ninette de Valois for a
ballet produced at Sadler's Wells Theatre, and it

seems to be regaining popularity judging by radio programmes. Here again the wistful quality of which I have spoken is strongly represented in the *Aubade, The Serious Doll, The Sad Doll* and the interlude, *Dreaming*, which precedes the final movement *Envoi*. But in this work the composer is no longer young and the whole work is, to my ear, that of an old man rather wistfully trying to recall the emotions and dreams of his youth. And no wonder, for the composer's letters recently published have shown how very disillusioned and changed he was at this time about many things he had formerly held dear.

Elgar seems never to have set out to write a waltz but much of his most characteristic light music is in 3/8 time and is what the world of light music describes as a valsette. Characteristic examples are his *Sérénade lyrique* for small orchestra (1899); the second of his *Dream Children*; and the first part of *The Dance of the Nautch Girls* from his *Crown of India*. *The Sad Doll* from the *Nursery Suite* is in slow waltz time.

In all this light music I have mentioned, the composer's orchestration is of the same masterly kind as in his greatest works—the Symphonies, the Concertos, *The Dream of Gerontius*. Every mark that the orchestral player could want —expression, phrasing, bowing—is written there with the sure hand of the master orchestrator.

But the conductor must approach it with the simple eye and heart of the young if its real beauty is to be brought out. The " great " conductor who lives only in the rarified air of symphonies, oratorios and the more austere operas may find these little pieces too elusive; but they contain much of the essential Elgar, and English music would be the poorer for lack of them.

STANFORD ROBINSON

A Modern View

MANY people will wish during the year 1957 to write about Edward Elgar to mark the centenary of his birth. The majority of the writers will doubtless belong to a generation born before the first World War—some, indeed, will look back with nostalgia to the peaceful Edwardian era, and some even to the late Victorian years. There may be a few among them who enjoyed Elgar's friendship and who witnessed the creation of some of his music. They can write with the authority which springs from knowledge.

But it is fitting also that some of those born after the composer had produced his last complete major work—the Cello Concerto (1919)—should be able to pay their humble tribute to one who not only greatly enriched the store of English music, but who penetrated, with the *Enigma Variations,* the international barriers.

To many younger musicians who never knew him as a man, Elgar remains a problem, for there seem, in fact, to be two Elgars. There is Elgar No. 1, the man of genius who could give the world *The Dream of Gerontius, The Apostles, The Kingdom,* the *Enigma Variations,* the *Introduction and Allegro,* the Symphonies, the Concertos for Violin and

Violoncello, *Falstaff*, and many smaller works which bear the mark of inspiration.

Then there is Elgar No. 2, who could plumb the depths of banality in some of his works, with wearisome melodic sequences, harmonies of mawkish sentimentality, and at times blatant vulgarity.

It seems incredible to the younger generation that the man who could express in *Gerontius* such nobility and rare poetic feeling, could in the same breath utter the trite language of the drawing-room ballads. To make the problem more complex, we are told that he sincerely believed in the value of his " popular " music and that he treated it almost as seriously as the work which today we recognize as great.

Elgar No. 2 has been dying for many years, and his passing in this centenary year would evoke little grief.

Elgar No. 1, on the other hand—the Elgar of those fertile twenty years from 1899 to 1919— will assuredly live. The strength and vitality of that existence will depend mainly upon two factors:

(1) The intelligent understanding shown by future conductors, singers and players of the style required to fulfil the composer's intentions. The music of Elgar, which demands flexibility of rhythm, subtlety of phrasing, and unusual

attention to problems of balance, owing to the complexity of the texture, can suffer perhaps more than that of any other English composer through a lack of sympathy and sensitivity on the part of the executants.

(2) The degree to which performers and audiences are prepared to study the works in detail.

It is possible, for example, to enjoy a performance of *The Dream of Gerontius*, *The Apostles* and *The Kingdom* without being conscious of Elgar's use of Leitmotiv, just as it is possible to enjoy Milton's Paradise Lost without understanding the classical allusions, or to admire the west façade of Wells Cathedral without being fully aware of the Gothic detail. The beauty and power of the music can make a direct appeal, just as can the majesty of the Miltonic language, or the splendour of a cathedral edifice. But the full enjoyment of the great choral and orchestral works comes as the reward of detailed study, without which the dramatic significance of the thematic allusions cannot be appreciated.

The laws of nature proclaim both change and evolution. As surely as winter follows summer, so do musical fashions change. It is not surprising, therefore, that the opulent sonority of Elgar's music should have yielded in the present generation to a terser and more

astringent form of expression, reflecting the increased pace and tension of modern life. Neither is it surprising that the harmonic vocabulary should have been enlarged, that composers should have displayed greater rhythmical ingenuity and even eschewed the accepted tonality in their search for new modes of self-expression.

That Elgar's music should have held its place in the cathedrals, concert-halls and recital rooms of this country as it has done during the last thirty years is proof, if proof were required, of the abiding value of his best works.

The little village of Broadheath and the city of Worcester can think with especial pride and thankfulness during this centenary year of the man who became one of England's greatest musicians.

DAVID WILLCOCKS

Elgar as a Man of Letters

Biography is a paradoxical occupation. To write of the living, or of those whom one has known in life, is almost impossible; in respect of the dead, whether illustrious or not, the task is easier. For, provided sufficient evidence is forthcoming, one may learn the character of the subject intimately, and free from prejudices and affections which may arise in personal relationships and lead to miscalculation. Biographies may be enthusiastic, derogatory, or objective, and outstanding examples of each exist. But a work of biography reaches its highest level when sympathy, in its fullest meaning, is most evident.

The absolutists will not have it that music can describe. A generation or two ago, however, it was considered that characters could be portrayed through music no less effectively than through words, and there is ample evidence to support this thesis. For instance, what more can be said of Tristan and Isolde than is said by Wagner? And does not Strauss add to our knowledge of Don Quixote or Elgar of Falstaff?

Here is a crucial point. *Falstaff* is regarded generally as one of Elgar's noblest achievements —not because it is formally beyond reproach, not because it is better orchestrated than any other of

his works, but because it evinces a state of sympathy to which few may aspire. "I love," wrote Charles Lamb somewhere, "to lose myself in other men's minds." In *Falstaff,* palpably, that is what Elgar did. One begins to see, without further consideration, the capacity for biography that Elgar possessed. By an accident of environment, however, his genius was turned into the channel of music. From his father, from his uncle, he acquired a technique which would be serviceable in the family business: it was as simple as that. Elgar was not the first, but he was very nearly the last to take to music in this way.

Most of us from time to time are haunted by an *alter ego*—what we might have been. Elgar never quite escaped the other Elgar, who was a potential man of letters. The reasons are clear. On the one hand he loved books, on the other he was sensitive to the calumny—which aggravated the more as time went on—that he was lacking in those qualities formerly thought to be as respectable as they were necessary to a middle-class "man of culture". (There is still to be detected, I suspect, a certain malodour in our native musical affairs derived from the solemn irrelevancies of two generations ago.)

The injustice of the calumny hurt terribly. It is only necessary to turn to an almost savage outburst in an otherwise urbane and beautifully

written introduction to Hubert Leicester's *Forgotten Worcester* (1930): " From among the crudities which one of the many—why are there so many?—unbrilliant university men has used in reference to myself, the following comes to mind. I am said to have ' left the humdrum atmosphere of Worcester for '—etc. I object to this."

The private Elgar, as shown in his correspondence, reveals how wide of the mark were those who sneered at his alleged lack of cultural competence. As a theologian (what reading went into the oratorios!) he would have sailed through whatever papers in church history are set for ordination candidates. His knowledge of architecture was thorough. He had an eye for good paintings. His acquaintance with European literature, whether ancient or modern, was so extensive as to put to shame those of us who study his writings from the little eminence of a university course in English Literature.

It was Francis Bacon who defined wonder as the seed of knowledge—and wonder was the particular quality of the Romantic school to which, by temperament and in point of time, Elgar belonged. Wonder, too, is the mark of the child; and one of the engaging features of Elgar was his perpetual resolve never to forget the virtues and visions of youth.

In his music there are a dozen or so pieces which must rank among the most charming illuminations of the child world; in his letters a continual reaching back to the prime sources of inspiration and pleasure. Almost his last thoughts—as dictated from his deathbed to Florence Norbury—were of the early pattern of life in the sunlit meadows between Teme and Severn.

It seemed an affront to some that Elgar was "self-educated", to others that he was "provincial". In the long run he proved that self-education was a very good form of education, and that in the provinces there was for the imaginative an inexhaustible store of wisdom. One of the most moving features of Elgar's character was his abiding loyalty to his roots: to be a Freeman of the City of Worcester was the real summit of ambition.

In the professional sense Elgar was not a philosopher; but, as I read him, he pursued truth with such pertinacity that the shape of ultimate wisdom was not far beyond his reach. (That provocative partner intuition tells me that this is the glory of *Gerontius,* and Elgar himself assures me in his end note: ". . . but this I saw and knew; this if anything is worth your memory.") His pursuit brought pain and suffering, disillusionment and discontent—the outward marks

that were noted by his contemporaries. But inwardly he was aware of a spiritual unity that transcended yet embraced men and women, their actions, their thoughts, their environment. Elgar's religious convictions have often been treated with less than justice. He was this, and then was not; therefore he was an apostate. But the fact is that the religious truths which he was taught by his parents—those " two honest old burghers " as he referred to them—remained in essence constant. This was confirmed by Elgar himself when, as late as 1926, he confirmed the theological motive which in his youth had set him towards his intended trilogy of oratorios. A canon having taken exception to the music of Wagner being performed in Worcester cathedral, Elgar wrote a letter to the local evening paper. In this he said: " The doctrine of repentance and forgiveness does not seem to be within the Canon's vision . . . ; if [he] bans Wagner from the services of the church, he must, if he is logical, cast out David and others. As to the ' delirium of sensual love and that craving for the ministrations of the white-robed angels ', has the Canon forgotten John Donne who, after experiencing the same travail, ended his life as a Dean in the same Church of England of which Canon Lacey is such a distinguished, if a some-what disingenuous ornament? "

So would have spoken either of the " two honest burghers ", who were no more inclined to periphrasis than their son.

Much as he would have liked to have been a public writer—and, once or twice, he sallied forth as such—Elgar's intimate papers are the essential documents: not because they are sensational, but precisely because they are not. From the literary forum into which he ventured there remain a couple of learned essays—which were printed in the correspondence columns of *The Times Literary Supplement,* introductions to three books (one on singing by David Ffrangçon-Davies, the second a primer on notation, and the third, Hubert Leicester's enchanting sheaf of essays), and a few programme notes. Here, as often in public, Elgar played his convincing, if misleading, part as the man who could do what others did, but better. The countryman could be a courtier with the rest, the untutored man from the west country a scholar among scholars. There was histrionic talent in the family, and Elgar could make good use of it as a defensive armour.

Once, at the height of his fame, he wrote to his friend—perhaps his most intimate and understanding friend—Troyte Griffith: " Although I have, much against my will, developed into a busy man since we first met, I do not cease to have the same warm feelings towards you and

think over your affairs and conversations as much as ever." *Plus ça change, plus c'est la même chose.*

Letters to friends are casual affairs, and not as a rule written with an eye on posterity. They are about small issues—the changing of a library book, the behaviour of a pet dog, the itinerary of a summer holiday, the supply of refreshments for a concert party. Yet it is, as Edward Holmes remarks in his *Life of Mozart,* the small things that tell us most about a man. Thus Elgar emerges as an integrated character from his letters to the Webbs of Worcester; to Francis Reeve, his old schoolmaster; to his family; to C. W. Buck, the Yorkshire country doctor whose early insistence on Elgar's genius was so great a spur; to Troyte Griffith, architect and painter; to the Schusters; to " Dorabella ". . . . We are fortunate that so many evidences of his affection for, and trust in, people remain.

It sometimes appears a safe axiom that a great artist is egocentric. In the present case the term is deprived of its customary derogatory reference by countless instances of warm-heartedness. How hard Elgar worked that his friends—Alban Claughton, son of a cathedral dignitary who had once espoused the cause of Elgar, Ivor Atkins, Percy Hull, Walford Davies, Dan Godfrey, Granville Bantock—should be rewarded or honoured. Nor, as when Hugh Blair fell on evil

times, did he forget them in misfortune. As for his family they were always in mind. Frank Elgar, whose talent according to his brother was not inconsiderable, was ill for a long time in the late 1920s. Edward at once went to his aid, assisted his business affairs, and devoted much time to his entertainment. If his sister Helen, a Dominican nun, required music for her convent chapel at Stroud, or a new piano for the community, Edward supplied the first in his lucid manuscript and saw to it in respect of the second that the sisterhood obtained a bargain.

The sensitivity of Elgar is well known. It was, however, as often as not the distresses of others that touched his moods.

" After thirty-seven years," he wrote to Frank Schuster in the tragic spring of 1920, " my poor old sister may have to turn out [of her house near Bromsgrove]. All the consideration she was treated with as the widow of a respected (and beloved) manager of the salt works is thrown to the winds—so I am in a sad house: the same fate is due on May 1st for my poor old *eldest* sister— stone deaf, etc., her little house has been bought ' over their heads ' and she is turned out—no- where to go ! So you see I am unhappy. . . .

" Don't talk to me of achievement. I drank spider juice for my mother's sake, went thro' penurious times to buy my dear wife a

car for her old age. . . . But Juno's nose presses against me and says a walk is near."

The concluding sentence turns towards the one sure consolation. Elgar was no urban or academic nature-lover, made so by the doctrines of Romantic literature. He felt himself to be so much a part of nature that it may be said in no mere matter-of-fact way that his roots were deep in his native soil. Once, and only once, did nature seem almost to fail him. Thus he wrote soon after the death of Lady Elgar: "Inscrutable nature goes on just the same—young larks, six in a nest on the lawn and many other birds; nightingales sing; but I miss the gentlest presence and I cannot go on".

The character of a great man is a hostage to fortune. It is sometimes reshaped by those of later time according to a set pattern; hence the everyday corollary which comes out in the form —" he looks like a musician ". It is used as a guide to personal hopes and fears, as a yardstick by which to measure achievement and disappointment. So while acknowledging the greatness of the great it is tempting to look for the Achilles heel and to adopt that as a general phsychological index.

In this essay there has hitherto been no mention of Elgar's petulance, obstinacy, and frequent prejudice, nor (except by implication) of

his marked tendency to hypochondria. All of these are in his letters, but, in the long run, all of less consequence than the positive qualities assembled under the general term sympathy.

Among the immortals there must at this time be much talk about the *sublunary* celebrations with which the living pay a respect to the dead out of all proportion to what they received in life.

For those who like characters served up neat and tidy, numbered and labelled as clinical exhibits, Elgar is not their man. We end where we began—with a paradox, or (as must be inevitable) an enigma. But so are we all. Our hero thus becomes what perhaps he most desired to be, an ordinary man; which is as good a reason as any other for his becoming an extraordinary musician.

PERCY M. YOUNG

SET IN 12 POINT SPECTRUM, 2 POINT LEADED
PRINTED AND BOUND IN GREAT BRITAIN BY
NOVELLO AND COMPANY LTD.
LONDON W.I